150.

Ber

D0435949

DO SOMETHING BESIDES WATCH T.V.

What to do when your mom or dad says . . .
"DO SOMETHING BESIDES WATCHING TV!"

By
JOY WILT BERRY

Living Skills Press
Fallbrook, California

Distributed by:

Word, Incorporated
4800 W. Waco Drive
Waco, TX 76703

CREDITS

Producer
  Ron Berry

Editor
  Orly Kelly

Weekly Reader Books edition published by
arrangement with Living Skills Press.

Dear Parents,

Most children are endowed with abundant supplies of mental and physical energy. This energy often seeks its release through activity and involvement. For this reason children have a tremendous need to **do something**. When they are bored, they often fulfill this need by doing something that is unacceptable. Thus, boredom can result in misbehavior.

Parents who discover this fact are often intimidated by it. All too often they assume the responsibility for a child's boredom so that they will not have to deal with its possible negative consequences. These parents choose to entertain their children so that their children will not misbehave.

At first glance, this may seem to be a wise thing to do, but in reality it is not. Children whose parents entertain them usually become dependent in unhealthy ways. They depend on their parents to program their lives, and they become frustrated and even angry if their parents should at some point fail to do so. Unfortunately, these children never learn to deal with their boredom in creative, productive ways.

The responsibility for a child's boredom must be shifted from the parent to the child if this predicament is to be avoided. This transfer will be easier if both parents and children realize that —

- boredom can be positive if it results in children's doing positive things; and

- children benefit most from the experiences that they, themselves, initiate and implement.

DO SOMETHING BESIDES WATCHING TV! helps children to realize these things. In addition, it motivates them into responsibility toward themselves and tells them exactly what they should do whenever they are bored.

It is my hope that children who understand and integrate the contents of this book into their everyday lives will become more productive and will never have to hear their parents say to them, "DO SOMETHING BESIDES WATCHING TV!"

Sincerely,

Joy Wilt Berry

Has your mother or father ever told you to...

Whenever your parents tell you to do something, do you ever wonder...

If any of this sounds familiar to you, you are going to **love** this book!

Because it will tell you what to do when you think that there is nothing to do.

BOREDOM

When there is nothing interesting or exciting for you to do, you might become BORED.

When you are bored, you might begin to think that you and your life are dreary and dull.

To overcome your boredom you might decide
to do something DESTRUCTIVE.

If you should do this, you will get yourself in trouble. This is not good. Never do anything that would hurt another person or yourself. Do not do anything that would damage or destroy someone's things.

When you are bored, you should not expect someone else to come up with something for you to do.

It is up to you to make your life interesting and exciting. When you are bored, you must decide what you are going to do. It is your responsibility to handle your own boredom.

TAKING CARE OF YOUR RESPONSIBILITIES

When you are bored and need to think of something to do, ask yourself this question:

Decide whether there are any UNFINISHED CHORES you need to do. It may be helpful to keep a list of the chores you are supposed to do so that you can go over the list whenever you are bored.

Decide whether there are PROMISES you
need to fulfill. Try to remember if you have done
everything that you promised other people you
would do.

Decide whether there are PERSONAL NEEDS you should take care of. Try to remember if there is anything you need to do for yourself. Should you wash your hair or clean your nails? Try to remember if there is anything you need to do to take care of your things. Should you feed your pets, wash your clothes or polish your shoes?

If you have chores, promises or personal needs that should be taken care of, DO THEM **BEFORE** YOU DO ANYTHING ELSE!

AVOID PROCRASTINATING. This means, don't wait until later. Take care of your chores, promises and personal needs immediately so that you can go on to do something that you want to do. You will enjoy doing the things you want to do much more if you do not feel that there are things you should be doing instead.

PLANNING THINGS TO DO

Once you have fulfilled your responsibilities, you are ready to put together some activities for yourself to do.

Begin by asking yourself:

Once you have decided whom you want to be with, talk with the person. Ask if he or she can get together with you. Be sure that it is all right with your parents before you make any final plans.

If you are able to be with another person, you can make plans together. If you cannot be with another person, you will have to be alone.

It is not bad for you to be alone. In fact, there might be times when you may choose to be alone. Being alone can be relaxing and fun if you do the right things.

Once it is decided whether you will be alone or with someone, ask yourself a second question:

If you do not want to stay at home, try to think of places you could go. Think about riding your bike or walking somewhere. It is a good idea to talk with your parents about this. Together you can make a list of the places to which you may walk or ride your bike. If there aren't places close enough to you, or if it is too dangerous for you to go someplace alone, you will need to have an adult go with you or take you. If there is no adult to do this, you need to stay home.

If you decide to stay home, you will need to
think some more. Are you going to be outside?

Are you going to be inside?

Once you have decided where you will be, ask yourself a third question:

You may choose to do something that is PHYSICAL. With physical activity, you would use your body.

You may choose to do something that is MENTAL. With mental activity, you would use your mind.

You may choose to do something that is PASSIVE. A passive activity would not require you to use your body or your mind. It would allow you to rest and relax.

Here are some PHYSICAL ACTIVITIES you can do alone if you are OUTSIDE:

- Walk, jog, take a hike.
- Play a sport (hit a tennis ball against a backboard, shoot baskets, etc.).
- Ride a bike, skateboard or go-cart.
- Fly a kite.
- Jump a rope.
- Play a game (jacks, hopscotch, etc.).
- Practice throwing a Frisbee, etc.
- Build something (with wood and nails, etc.).

If you find friends, you can do all of the above plus playing sports like soccer, tennis, or catch.

Can you think of other physical activities you can do outside?

Make your own list.

SKATEBOARD

FLY A KITE

HiKE

JUMP ROPE

Here are some PHYSICAL ACTIVITIES you can do alone if you are INSIDE:

- Do some exercises.
- Dance.
- Pretend to be something — act it out.
- Play hopscotch (with tape lines on the floor, with your parents' permission).
- Build a hideout or fort (with furniture, sheets, boxes, etc.).
- Fly paper airplanes (but only in a room where nothing can be knocked over).

If you find friends, you can do all of the above plus body games like Twister, Simon Says, Can You Do This? and Follow The Leader.

Can you think of other physical activities you can do inside?

Make your own list.

Here are some MENTAL ACTIVITIES you can do alone if you are OUTSIDE:

- Do an art project that may be too messy to do inside (work with paint, clay, papier-mâché, etc.).
- Observe something (like an insect). Look at it closely. Watch it carefully. See what you can learn about it.
- Look around. Try to see things that you never noticed before.
- Listen. Note how many different sounds you can hear.
- Smell. Note how many different odors you can smell.
- Collect things (like rocks, shells, leaves).
- Do a scientific experiment that may be too messy to do inside.
- Think about the environment. Decide how you could improve it.

Can you think of other mental activities you can do outside?

Make your own list.

Here are some MENTAL ACTIVITIES you can do alone if you are INSIDE:

- Read.
- Play a game (solitaire, etc.).
- Work with a puzzle, riddle, cipher or code, or make up your own.
- Do an art project using crayons, colored pens, pencils, etc.
- Cook something.
- Mend or sew something.
- Write something (a story, letter, diary entry, etc.).
- Make something with things you can find around the house.

If you find friends, you can do all of the above plus games like chess, checkers, Monopoly, etc.

Can you think of other mental activities you can do inside?

Make your own list.

Here are some PASSIVE THINGS you can do alone if you are OUTSIDE:

- Lie on your back, look up in the sky and watch the clouds move.
- Find a quiet place to be alone and to sit quietly.
- Sunbathe.
- Lie in the grass, close your eyes and let your mind wander.

Can you think of other passive things you can do outside?

Make your own list.

Here are some PASSIVE THINGS you can do alone if you are INSIDE:

- Listen to music.
- Daydream.
- Take a nap.
- Lie on your back. Concentrate on relaxing your body.

Can you think of other passive things you can do inside?

Make up your own list.

DOING SOMETHING ABOUT BOREDOM

The main questions that you have read in this book should be written on a piece of paper and kept in a handy place. Whenever you are bored, read each question and answer it. This will help you to overcome your boredom.

Here are the questions that need to be included in your list:

So that you don't have to rethink every issue each time you are bored, make yourself three lists. Keep these lists by the four questions.

One list should include your CHORES.

A second list should include PLACES TO GO when you want to be away from home.

A third list should include THINGS TO DO.
Be sure to write down —

- **PHYSICAL ACTIVITIES** to do outside;
- **PHYSICAL ACTIVITIES** to do inside;

- **MENTAL ACTIVITIES** to do outside;
- **MENTAL ACTIVITIES** to do inside;

- **PASSIVE ACTIVITIES** to do outside;
- **PASSIVE ACTIVITIES** to do inside.

When you are making up your lists, do not include any activity that would hurt other people or cause you to hurt yourself. And do not include any activity that would damage or destroy property.

Try to think of things to do that will make you a better person and will help the people around you.

THE END of watching too much TV!